DINOSAUR FACT DIG

BRACHIOSAURUS
AND OTHER LONG-NECKED DINOSAURS

THE NEED-TO-KNOW FACTS

BY
REBECCA RISSMAN

Consultant: Mathew J. Wedel, PhD
Associate Professor
Western University of Health Services

Raintree is an imprint of Capstone Global Library Limited, a company incorporated in England and Wales having its registered office at 264 Banbury Road, Oxford, OX2 7DY – Registered company number: 6695582

www.raintree.co.uk
myorders@raintree.co.uk

Edited by Michelle Hasselius
Designed by Kazuko Collins
Picture research by Wanda Winch
Production by Gene Bentdahl

ISBN 978 1 474 71938 4 (hardcover)
20 19 18 17 16
10 9 8 7 6 5 4 3 2 1

ISBN 978 1 474 71951 3 (paperback)
21 20 19 18 17
10 9 8 7 6 5 4 3 2 1

British Library Cataloguing in Publication Data
A full catalogue record for this book is available from the British Library.

ACKNOWLEDGEMENTS
All images by Jon Hughes except: MapArt (maps), Shuttershock: Elena Elisseeva, green gingko leaf, Jiang Hongyan, yellow gingko leaf, Taigi, paper background

Every effort has been made to contact copyright holders of material reproduced in this book. Any omissions will be rectified in subsequent printings if notice is given to the publisher.

All the internet addresses (URLs) given in this book were valid at the time of going to press. However, due to the dynamic nature of the internet, some addresses may have changed, or sites may have changed or ceased to exist since publication. While the author and publisher regret any inconvenience this may cause readers, no responsibility for any such changes can be accepted by either the author or the publisher.

Printed and bound in China.

CONTENTS

WAS THAT AN EARTHQUAKE?

No! That's the booming sound of Brachiosaurus and other long-necked dinosaurs walking. These plant-eating giants lived between 210 and 65 million years ago. They roamed in forests, plains and coastal areas. Learn more about Brachiosaurus and other enormous dinosaurs, such as Argentinosaurus, Cetiosauriscus and Rhoetosaurus.

AGUSTINIA

PRONOUNCED: AG-us-TIN-ee-a

NAME MEANING: named after Agustin Martinelli, who found the first Agustinia fossils

TIME PERIOD LIVED: Early Cretaceous Period, 115 to 100 million years ago

LENGTH: 15 metres (50 feet)

WEIGHT: 8 metric tons (8.8 tons)

TYPE OF EATER: herbivore

PHYSICAL FEATURES: long neck and tail, thick body

AGUSTINIA lived alongside other long-necked herbivores, such as Limaysaurus.

Only a few **AGUSTINIA** bones have been discovered.

Agustinia lived in the forests
of what is now Argentina.

N

W ←◆→ E

S

where this
dinosaur
lived

Paleontologists first thought
AGUSTINIA had long, spiny plates on
its back. But these bones were from
another part of the dinosaur's body.

APATOSAURUS

PRONOUNCED: a-PAT-oh-SAWR-us

NAME MEANING: deceptive reptile, because fossils look like bones from Mosasaur, an ancient water reptile

TIME PERIOD LIVED: Late Jurassic Period, about 150 million years ago

LENGTH: 26 metres (85 feet)

WEIGHT: 32 metric tons (35 tons)

TYPE OF EATER: herbivore

PHYSICAL FEATURES: long neck and tail

APATOSAURUS had the widest neck of any dinosaur.

Paleontologists do not think **APATOSAURUS** lived in herds. The dinosaur's fossils are often found alone.

Apatosaurus lived in North America.

N
W E
S

■ where this dinosaur lived

APATOSAURUS swallowed its food whole.

ARGENTINOSAURUS

PRONOUNCED: ARE-jen-TEEN-oh-SAW-rus

NAME MEANING: Argentina lizard

TIME PERIOD LIVED: middle Cretaceous Period, about 100 million years ago

LENGTH: 30 metres (100 feet)

WEIGHT: 74 metric tons (82 tons)

TYPE OF EATER: herbivore

PHYSICAL FEATURES: one of the largest dinosaurs that ever lived, legs as large as tree trunks

ARGENTINOSAURUS' eggs were the size of American footballs.

Argentinosaurus lived in the forests and plains of what is now Argentina.

N
W E
S

■ where this dinosaur lived

It took 40 years for **ARGENTINOSAURUS** to reach full size.

ARGENTINOSAURUS had the longest legs of any known dinosaur. Its thighbones were 2.5 meters (8 feet) long.

BRACHIOSAURUS

PRONOUNCED: BRACK-ee-oh-SAWR-us

NAME MEANING: arm lizard

TIME PERIOD LIVED: Late Jurassic Period, about 150 million years ago

LENGTH: 26 metres (85 feet)

WEIGHT: 23 metric tons (25 tons)

TYPE OF EATER: herbivore

PHYSICAL FEATURES: long neck, small feet for its size

BRACHIOSAURUS ate ferns and tree leaves all day.

BRACHIOSAURUS had a longer neck and shorter tail than most other long-necked dinosaurs.

Brachiosaurus lived in
North America.

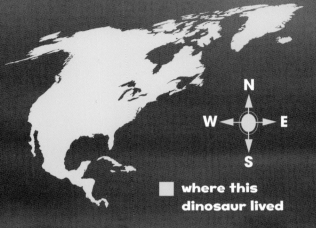

N
W E
S

■ where this
dinosaur lived

The dinosaur's ribs were
more than 2.1 metres
(7 feet) long.

BRACHYTRACHELOPAN

PRONOUNCED: BRACK-i-tratch-eh-LOW-pan

NAME MEANING: short-neck shepherd god; fossils were discovered by a shepherd named Daniel Mesa

TIME PERIOD LIVED: Late Jurassic Period, about 150 million years ago

LENGTH: 11 metres (35 feet)

WEIGHT: 5 metric tons (5.5 tons)

TYPE OF EATER: herbivore

PHYSICAL FEATURES: long tail, small head and short neck

BRACHYTRACHELOPAN could not reach tall trees. The dinosaur ate low-growing plants on the ground.

Brachytrachelopan lived in
what is now Argentina.

N

W ←→ E

S

where this
dinosaur
lived

BRACHYTRACHELOPAN may have
swung its tail like a whip to protect
itself from predators.

BRACHYTRACHELOPAN was
one of the smallest sauropods.

CAMARASAURUS

PRONOUNCED: KAM-uh-ruh-SAWR-us

NAME MEANING: chambered lizard

TIME PERIOD LIVED: Late Jurassic Period, about 150 to 145 million years ago

LENGTH: 15 metres (50 feet)

WEIGHT: 15 metric tons (16.5 tons)

TYPE OF EATER: herbivore

PHYSICAL FEATURES: long neck and tail, small head

CAMARASAURUS is named for the air-filled spaces in its backbone.

A young CAMARASAURUS skeleton is one of the most complete dinosaur skeletons ever found. It was discovered in 1925.

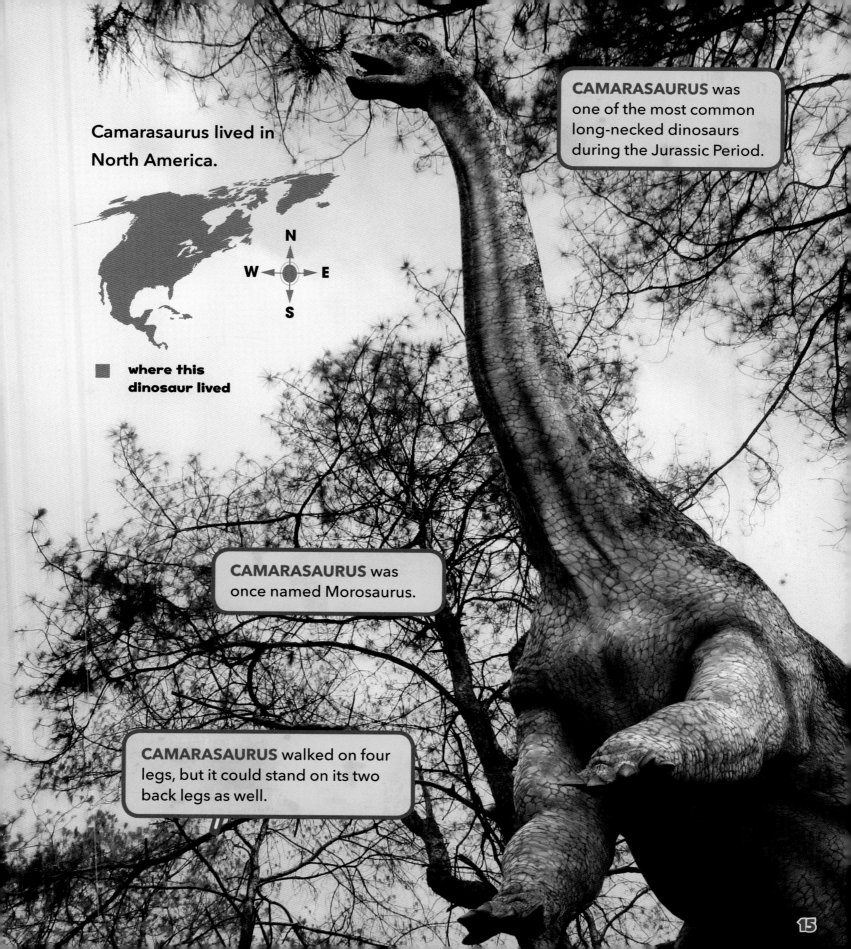

Camarasaurus lived in North America.

N
W ← ● → E
S

■ where this dinosaur lived

CAMARASAURUS was one of the most common long-necked dinosaurs during the Jurassic Period.

CAMARASAURUS was once named Morosaurus.

CAMARASAURUS walked on four legs, but it could stand on its two back legs as well.

CETIOSAURISCUS

PRONOUNCED: SEE-tee-oh-sawr-ISS-kus

NAME MEANING: like whale lizard

TIME PERIOD LIVED: Middle Jurassic Period, about 175 to 160 million years ago

LENGTH: 15 metres (50 feet)

WEIGHT: 4 metric tons (4.4 tons)

TYPE OF EATER: herbivore

PHYSICAL FEATURES: strong legs, small head and long tail

CETIOSAURISCUS had pencil-shaped teeth that pulled leaves off trees.

CETIOSAURISCUS was less than half the length of the longest dinosaurs.

Cetiosauriscus lived in the forests of what is now England.

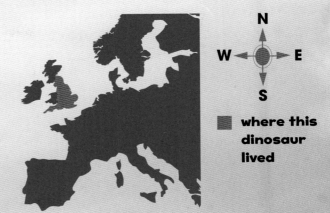

N
W · E
S

where this dinosaur lived

CETIOSAURISCUS whipped its tail from side to side to protect itself from predators.

Only two CETIOSAURISCUS skeletons have ever been found.

DIPLODOCUS

PRONOUNCED: di-PLO-doh-kus

NAME MEANING: double-beamed

TIME PERIOD LIVED: Late Jurassic Period, about 150 million years ago

LENGTH: 27 metres (90 feet)

WEIGHT: 11 to 14 metric tons (12 to 15 tons)

TYPE OF EATER: herbivore

PHYSICAL FEATURES: row of small, pointed scales on its back

DIPLODOCUS ate leaves from plants near the ground. It swallowed the leaves whole.

Diplodocus lived in North America.

N
W E
S

■ where this dinosaur lived

DIPLODOCUS was named after the double-beamed shape of its tailbones.

DIPLODOCUS was long but didn't weigh much more than a large elephant.

HUABEISAURUS

PRONOUNCED: HOO-ah-bay-SAWR-us

NAME MEANING: north China lizard, because fossils were discovered in northern China

TIME PERIOD LIVED: Late Cretaceous Period, about 75 million years ago

LENGTH: 17 metres (55 feet)

WEIGHT: 8.5 metric tons (9.4 tons)

TYPE OF EATER: herbivore

PHYSICAL FEATURES: very long neck and tail, large body and small head

HUABEISAURUS fossils were discovered in 2000.

Like many large dinosaurs, HUABEISAURUS had to eat all day. It needed a lot of food to keep its huge body moving.

Huabeisaurus lived in what is now China.

■ where this dinosaur lived

N
W ⊕ E
S

Paleontologists believe the only **HUABEISAURUS** fossils that have been found are from a young dinosaur. They think an adult could have been even bigger.

OMEISAURUS

PRONOUNCED: OH-mee-SAWR-us

NAME MEANING: Omei lizard, because fossils were found at Omei Shan Mountain in China

TIME PERIOD LIVED: Late Jurassic Period, about 169 to 159 million years ago

LENGTH: 15 to 18 metres (50 to 60 feet)

WEIGHT: 5 to 8.5 metric tons (5.5 to 9.4 tons)

TYPE OF EATER: herbivore

PHYSICAL FEATURES: strong and sturdy legs, long neck and tail

OMEISAURUS had 17 bones in its neck. Today's giraffes have seven neck bones.

Many **OMEISAURUS** fossils were found in the 1970s and 1980s.

Omeisaurus lived what is now China.

where this dinosaur lived

OMEISAURUS stood on its back legs to reach leaves on high branches.

RHOETOSAURUS

PRONOUNCED: ROH-tuh-SAWR-us

NAME MEANING: Rhoetos lizard; Rhoetos was a mythical Greek giant

TIME PERIOD LIVED: Middle Jurassic Period, about 165 million years ago

LENGTH: 17 metres (55 feet)

WEIGHT: 20 metric tons (22 tons)

TYPE OF EATER: herbivore

PHYSICAL FEATURES: long tail and strong legs

A complete **RHOETOSAURUS** skeleton has never been found.

Rhoetosaurus lived in what is now Australia.

N
W ← → E
S

■ where this dinosaur lived

People first thought **RHOETOSAURUS** bones were from a circus elephant.

RHOETOSAURUS could walk about 15 kilometres (9 miles) per hour.

SALTASAURUS

PRONOUNCED: SAWL-tuh-SAWR-us

NAME MEANING: lizard from Salta; fossils were discovered in Salta, Argentina

TIME PERIOD LIVED: Late Cretaceous Period, about 70 to 65 million years ago

LENGTH: 8 metres (25 feet)

WEIGHT: 2 metric tons (2.2 tons)

TYPE OF EATER: herbivore

PHYSICAL FEATURES: wide body, plates shaped like spikes along its back

SALTASAURUS was the first armoured long-necked dinosaur to be discovered.

Saltasaurus lived in what is now Argentina.

N
W E
S

where this dinosaur lived

SALTASAURUS' neck bones are shaped like an owl's neck bones.

SALTASAURUS was about one-third the size of most long-necked dinosaurs.

SUUWASSEA

PRONOUNCED: SOO-wuss-SEE-ah

NAME MEANING: ancient thunder

TIME PERIOD LIVED: Late Jurassic Period, about 151 million years ago

LENGTH: 15 metres (50 feet)

WEIGHT: 10 metric tons (11 tons)

TYPE OF EATER: herbivore

PHYSICAL FEATURES: strong legs, small head and a short tail

SUUWASSEA had tall backbones. These bones might have formed a hump or short sail on the dinosaur's back.

SUUWASSEA fossils were found on the Native American Crow tribe's territory.

Suuwassea lived in what is now the United States.

where this dinosaur lived

SUUWASSEA lived and travelled in herds to stay safe from predators.

SUUWASSEA was small compared with other long-necked dinosaurs.

GLOSSARY

ANCIENT from a long time ago

ARMOUR bones, scales and skin that some animals have on their bodies for protection

CRETACEOUS PERIOD third period of the Mesozoic Era; the Cretaceous Period was from 145 to 65 million years ago

FERN plant with feathery leaves and no flowers; ferns usually grow in damp places

FOSSIL remains of an animal or plant from millions of years ago that have turned to rock

HERBIVORE animal that eats only plants

HERD group of the same kind of animal that live and travel together

JURASSIC PERIOD second period of the Mesozoic Era, the Jurassic Period was from 200 to 145 million years ago

PALEONTOLOGIST scientist who studies fossils

PLAIN large, flat area of land with few trees

PLATE flat, bony growth

PREDATOR animal that hunts other animals for food

PRONOUNCE say a word in a certain way

SCALE small piece of hard skin

SPIKE sharp, pointy object; many dinosaurs used their bony spikes to defend themselves

COMPREHENSION QUESTIONS

1. Agustin Martinelli discovered the first Agustinia fossils. What is a fossil?

2. Why did Brachytrachelopan eat low-growing plants?

3. What was the name of the first armoured long-necked dinosaur to be discovered?

READ MORE

Brachiosaurus (All About Dinosaurs), Dan Nunn (Raintree, 2014)

Brachiosaurus and other Long-necked Herbivores (Dinosaurs!), David West (Franklin Watts, 2013)

A Weekend with Dinosaurs (Fantasy Field Trips), Claire Throp (Raintree, 2014)

WEBSITES

www.bbc.co.uk/cbeebies/shows/andys-dinosaur-adventures

Go on a dinosaur adventure with Andy and Hatty! Play games, sing songs and watch clips all about dinosaurs.

www.show.me.uk/section/dinosaurs

This website has loads of fun things to do and see, including a dinosaur mask you can download and print, videos, games and Top Ten lists.

INDEX